Where the Poppies Grow

An anthology of poems about two World Wars

Ronald Cove

Ex Rifleman KRR/RB

www.dspublishingservices.co.uk

Denise Smith Publishing Services
167 Margate Road, Herne Bay
Kent CT6 7AB
www.dspublishingservices.co.uk

First published in the UK by Denise Smith Publishing Services, 2015

A CIP catalogue record for this book
is available from the British Library

ISBN: 978-0-9932639-0-3

Printed and bound in the UK by
Printdomain, 107 High Street, Thurnscoe
Rotherham, South Yorkshire S63 0QZ

Original photography by Denise Smith ©

Dedication

I dedicate this book to my dear late Mother who was an auxiliary nurse in the First World War, and my late Father-in-law, who would have appreciated these verses.

Acknowledgements

I would like to offer my thanks to a local artist and friend, Mike Stewart, for allowing me to put the painting of an early Rifleman in this book.

I would like to thank my wife for her patience in typing these verses and correcting my bad spelling. Also my daughter for taking the time to read each verse in order to see that they made sense.

I would also like to thank Nurse Althea Walker of Chestfield Medical Centre for introducing me to Denise Smith.

And last, but not least, I would like to thank Denise for putting so much work into bringing this book to print.

Introduction

First, let me say I have never considered myself to be a master poet. The reason I wrote these verses is quite simple: I had for many years harboured a number of stories that I was lucky enough to overhear when my father and his friends got together and would reminisce about their time spent together in the trenches in the Great War.

After many years of researching the Great War, I decided to write my first book based on these old soldiers' stories. This in turn led to a second and third book on the same subject, which I hasten to add no publisher has so far accepted! However, this brings me back to the first set of verses that I have set out here, about World War One.

I started writing verses when my daughter insisted on reading through each book, just to make sure they were in fact readable, and with my wife's help, correct any spelling mistakes that I admit were plentiful. Anyway, while waiting, I found myself at a loss. It therefore occurred to me that as I tried so hard to base my books on facts, I should now try writing a verse based on facts. Having lived in the East End of London throughout the blitz, I decided to write my first verse 'The Blitz'. Since then I have penned something like 80 more verses, several of which I am happy to say have been published in military journals.

Having served in two elite infantry regiments myself, 60th and 95th Rifles, I think it has given me some insight into how most soldiers would describe their feelings of fighting in a war, and I believe and hope that the following verses come near the mark. I have tried to add truth to each of the following verses. I hope you enjoy them.

Ronald Cove
Ex Rifleman KRRC/RB

To Ronald Cove

"There is great value in the writing of war poems and books. They serve to help us remember and commemorate the tremendous cost and sacrifice that all our servicemen and women endured. Your verses hold great weight, for which you should be commended."

Charles Byrne
Director of Fundraising
The Royal British Legion

Part 1 – First World War

WHERE THE POPPIES GROW

The sky was blue, the day so clear,
Each shell exploded much too near,
A whistle said it's over the top we must go,
To charge across a field, where only poppies grow.

Machine guns that had stood silent for a while,
Began to cut us down when in open file,
Many would never again see the sun's bright glow,
For they lay dead upon ground, where only poppies grow.

When so many failed to come back,
Others made ready for the next attack,
They charged across the same churned up ground,
Where only crushed poppies could now be found.

SILENT NIGHT
(*One Hundred Years 1914-2014*)

T'was Christmas Eve so long ago,
Our boys were fighting the common foe.

Suddenly as dark turned to light,
A lone voice started singing 'Silent Night'.

The song continued throughout that morn,
By men so tired and so forlorn.

Now Christmas Day had begun,
No-one fired a single gun.

Both sides met in no-man's land,
Where gifts were passed from man to man.

They greeted each other with a smiling face,
With a hope to vacate that awful place.

Alas, the Generals could stand it no more,
So ordered their men to resume the war.

Many more men had to die,
In that coming terrible fight.

For their Generals never heard,
That solitary voice singing 'Silent Night'.

HALLOWED GROUND

Here boys, can you hear our guns?
Why! They've got old Fritz on the run.

When each shell does explode,
With another they quickly load.

Look, there go our boys marching through,
Today there are so many, tomorrow there'll be just a few.

There go our Rifles into the attack,
But see old Fritz is still fighting back.

Now our machine guns will cut him down,
But none of this now worries us.

For we now rest in peace beneath this
Hallowed Ground.

THE LAST SUNRISE

Dear friend, did you see the sunrise?
Were you awake at dawn?
Were you in the same old trench?
Feeling alone and so forlorn.

Did you see that sunshine bright,
Bid farewell to that cold, black night?
Did you see our boys attack?
Were you sad when none came back?

Did you see that sunrise
Through cold, staring eyes?
Just to see another sunrise,
Tears would flow from my eyes.

Dear friend, did you see that sunrise
While lying on your feather bed?
Or are you lying in the mud
With me, cold, alone and dead?

REMEMBER THAT DAY

Remember that day
We went over the top,
The blood we spilt,
Not a single drop.

Remember that day,
Struggling with Boche barbed wire,
Then charging on through
That blood soaked mire.

Remember that day,
As each friend went down,
And just lay there
Without a sound.

Remember that day,
Oh, such a brilliant attack,
So bravely onward we charged,
Yet not one single soul ever came back.

ONES WE LOVE

In the dark of night,
A flare shone bright,
Will this slaughter never pass?
Must we fight till the last?

Our pain is raw,
Must we suffer ever more?
Our blood flows red,
So many men now lay dead.

Men's eyes now full of hate,
Except for those who lie and wait
For the Lord to greet them
At the golden gate.

Each man's soul is scarred by war,
They'll never be as they were before,
Will it end on that homeward train?
Or stay forever in each man's brain?

When the roll is called
High above,
Will we then be
With the ones we love?

LOST COMRADES

The sound of battle still fills the air,
It re-visits that trench you boys dug, just over there,
The spirit of dead comrades will give you a smile,
As you linger in silence, just for a while.

They will forever remember your name, your face,
Though you may forget when they died, and the place,
You will think of the comradeship, laughter and joy,
You had for a time when only a boy.

The day you went forward, you'll remember so well,
And those men going down as you walked into hell,
You'll reflect on those times on walking away,
And those left in that trench, now forever must stay.

Yes the sound of battle you'll remember so well,
And those young boys that were with you,
Who were cut down by machine gun and shell.

A LITTLE LEAD SOLDIER

Just a little lead soldier,
Which stood under a glass,
Who fought in that war,
The one before last.

He was dusted each morning.
With a clean yellow rag,
Never saying a word,
Not even to brag.

He just stood on the shelf,
So shiny and bright,
As though guarding us children,
By day and by night.

When I think of that little lead soldier,
I feel really sad,
For somehow he brings back memories,
Of my dear old Dad.

Although both these old soldiers,
Were not very tall,
To me they still are,
The bravest warriors of all.

A ROAD TO NOWHERE 1914-18

They walk a road that leads to nowhere,
Then they fight another battle again, somewhere.

After so much fighting they end up in some place,
To find they're alive but cannot remember a dead friend's face.

Then it's rest and move on once again,
Yet the ground they cover looks just the same.

Now it's pack up and move back,
And traverse the same familiar tracks.

By this time their friends are sadly all gone,
Nevertheless they will bravely fight on.

Because by this time no-one seems to care,
They are walking a road that leads to nowhere – 1939-45.

MADNESS OF WAR

Who's to say
how many more,
Shall be sacrificed,
In this terrible war?

For freedom, they say,
Our young men must die,
Yet for them this really,
Doesn't apply.

It's surely a crime,
For so many young men
To be cut down
While in their prime.

Freedom, democracy,
These words we cry,
Then send more young boys
Out only to die.

Have they no feelings at all,
Those men who sit in Whitehall?
For if they don't stop this thing they are doing,
It must surely end in this country's ruin.

So should we give,
Just one life more,
To the madness of
This unholy war?

1914 - DAY OF PEACE

Christmas morning found them in a frosty trench,
Dead comrades still tangled on that barbed wire fence.

When all across that blood soaked ground,
There came a soothing, haunting sound.

All weapons there were cast aside,
For no soldier that day had need to die.

Their voices rang out, so clear singing 'Silent Night',
But with the morn, as enemies, they resumed that bloody fight.

COURT MARTIAL

For cowardice he died,
Shot by one man and five,
The court martial did decide,
This young man had to die.

Yet his defence did insist,
Although the shell missed,
It had caused him to stray,
Not run away.

Where he suddenly found
Himself on the ground,
Overcome by an anxiety spell,
Caused by that very same shell.

Which made his mates fall,
Killing them all,
Yet his peers did decide,
Was just a tissue of lies.

So therefore you see,
We all do agree,
It's a firing squad,
We must now decree.

Then tied to a lone post,
By the men he did trust most,
Tommy silently died,
Shot down by one man and five.

DARKNESS

Each day has now merged into night,
Since that gas attack,
Cruelly robbed him of all sight.

Although he finds it so good to be safely back home,
Still darkness will surround him where ever he goes,
And each path he now walks, he walks all alone.

His wife's sweet smile he may never see again,
For he wanders the house,
With a brand new, white wooden cane.

Every friend's face he'd once known so well,
Must now live in memory,
Since that day he defied those awful gas shells.

OFFER A PRAYER

Was the year of our Lord nineteen-fourteen,
Our young men entered that war,
And many again would never be seen.

A generation of youngsters,
Marched into that Great War,
A generation of young boys, we never saw.

They fought in some rat-infested trench,
And charged across fields, only to be slaughtered,
When caught upon an enemy barbed wire fence.

Fighting an enemy who was far too strong,
While their loved ones at home,
Sang those old, war-time songs.

Today let us remember those lads full of joy,
As so proudly they marched off into war,
For they weren't yet men, they were only young boys.

Was for freedom they died, day after day,
Now in some far off battlefield,
Many Mothers' sons forever will stay.

So if you can find a minute to spare,
Think of what those boys must have gone through,
Then say 'thank-you' and offer a silent prayer.

A MOTHER'S TEARS

She cried with pride as he marched off to war,
She cried with sorrow when told he'd be home no more.

She cried when they carved his name in stone,
She cried because he still rests across the foam.

She cried for his wife and child,
She cried for these three all the while.

She cried alone each and every day,
She cried because that's the price a Mother must pay.

She cried for a son, his baby and wife,
She cried to the end of her own tormented life.

THE OLD SOLDIER'S PLIGHT

A lonely old soldier,
Who means no offence,
He now begs for a living,
And sleeps on a rickety park bench.

A loyal brave man,
Throughout the Great War,
Until he was wounded,
And could serve his country no more.

To throw him a penny,
Will do you no harm,
For this man fought on the Somme,
And there lost an arm.

Some people may say,
This crippled old cockney is a sight to behold,
Not knowing that he'd once been
A 60th Rifleman, one of the elite, 'Swift and Bold'.

There are those who will mock
This old soldier now shot to bits,
Yet, when of their age,
He stood twice as fit.

Although his fellow countrymen
Did cheer when he went off to war,
They now have no time for him,
And sadly his plight, they seem to ignore.

A BRITISH RIFLEMAN'S FRIEND

Was in Delhi as British lines fell,
They did side with the 60th Rifles,
To slay our enemy, like bats out of hell.

At that battle's end, the Rifles had found a new friend.
They came in answer to a fellow rifleman's call,
Because they are our friends, the Gurkha,
Born and bred in Nepal.

In many battles they have stood by our side,
To the 60th this comes as no real surprise,
For they are true soldiers of our Queen,
Who also dress in red, black and dark green.

MOTHER AND DAUGHTER

A young girl's heart pines
For the Father she never knew,
Her dear Mother hungers
For the man she loved so true.

This young girl is haunted
By a Father she had never met,
Her Mother still weeps
For the Lover she cannot forget.

The young girl wonders where
Her Father had gone,
For he promised her Mother
He wouldn't be very long.

One day, the war
Finally reached its sad end,
The Mother, for her daughter,
So tearfully did send.

Now within the chimes
Of a lone church bell,
She hugged her child,
And softly, this story did tell.

"My dear child, your Father's spirit
Is still here with us this day,
Although like every brave soldier,
His life just faded away.

"In Flanders he now lies,
Resting with friends in serene peace,
Yet for us dear child be sure,
His love never shall cease."

SACRIFICE

Now dawn is near,
Another battle we fear,
When will it be done,
And this war be won?

Must more men die,
While their loved ones cry?
How much more blood must be spilled,
Before our lust is stilled?

Why are we plagued with rats and lice?
Only to stay and be sacrificed,
To be placed in a grave with so many others,
Or will we awake from this dream to be greeted by dear Mothers?

WHEN THE BUTTERFLIES RETURN

There is a field where red poppies open wide,
To greet each friendly passing butterfly,
When in that field your bright blue eyes
Watch over me from out that deep blue sky.

In that field where all those poppies sway,
It seems all butterflies have now flown away,
Because so many men there still lay,
And with them dear, I fear I too must stay.

One day those poppies will re-bloom,
And butterflies will return through this gloom,
Although I'll still lie here with comrades true,
My spirit will forever walk with you.

GENERAL'S DILEMMA

We won't sleep so sound tonight,
For tomorrow there'll be a big fight,
The General will watch us go,
Then tell our Colonel
We're much too slow.

Our Captain yelling 'we must move faster',
Has Fritz falling over in fits of laughter.
As forward we run,
He'll give us a taste of his machine gun.

Men will go on if they are able,
Wishing their Captain wasn't so noble,
Reaching the enemy, what will we find?
He's fallen back, to the secondary line.

The Sergeant congratulates us with a pat on the back,
Then Fritz begins his counter attack,
His attack will be ever so bold,
Much too strong, we cannot hold.

Someone will say
It's a sticky wicket,
Everyone knows
We're not playing cricket.

Now this leaves our flank
High in the air,
Then the General will declare,
'Why can't Fritz play this game fair?'

So we're left in a field
Not feeling too smart,
All wishing we'd stayed
Back at the start.

FOR LOOS WE FIGHT

The sun comes up, the sun goes down,
Still bullets keep flying all around,
Each day the shells arrive from over there,
The men they kill have no more cares.

The lice still give a nasty nip,
When food comes up, rats will nick a bit.
No one's happy to be here,
We dream of home, and a nice cold beer.

We've held this line for just two days,
Will the enemy ever come? Well who can say,
For that town of Loos we fight once more,
Then we will count our dead by the score.

THE SOMME VALLEY

Many did die in that long bloody war,
Still the torment goes on,
For those that lived through,
That battle of the Somme.

T'was the first of July,
A day nice and clear,
With a bright blue sky,
Each whistle sounding so clear.

Men who marched so proud, so aloof,
Now rest in Flanders,
Cruelly robbed of their youth.

Some may have survived,
Yet their suffering goes on,
For these men well remember,
That valley of the Somme.

Yes, the flowers of England
Have sadly all gone,
They now sleep the long sleep,
In the shadow of the Valley by the Somme.

THEY CALLED HIM A COWARD

They called him a coward,
Said 'he's no good',
But on the spot where he fell,
Stands a cross made of wood.

Standing with comrades for each battle to win,
Always denying those demons he fought deep within,
When out of the line he still went through hell,
For of this fear, who could he tell?

Yes, they said he was a coward,
And really no good,
Yet still on that spot
Stands that cross made of wood.

THE GENTLEMEN GURKHA

To Delhi they first came,
As a gift sent from heaven,
To stand with the 60th rifles,
In the year of our Lord, 1857.

Was to be a critical battle,
Still they stayed by our side,
So their loyalty to Britain,
Cannot be denied.

With the 60th rifles they did stand,
True to our Queen,
Now these brave men from Nepal,
Do us an honour by wearing red on dark green.

Although it wasn't a must,
Yet from Delhi to this very day,
They have stood true to us,
Like any good friend, they fought through to the end.

Now there's a small part of heaven,
You will see if you try,
Where all riflemen go,
When they bid us goodbye.

But the part that shines brightest of all,
Is reserved for the 60th and their friends,
The Gurkha, who come from Nepal.

Yes these men that we speak of,
Would never think to desert us,
For they're every British riflemen's friend,
Those gentle riflemen, The Gurkhas.

A VISION

When I heard that battle cry,
A voice called to me from out the sky,
I knew it could be none other,
Than my dear departed Mother.

Charging forward with my mates,
It seemed death was to be my fate,
Suddenly a vision did appear,
T'was my loving wife, oh so clear.

As each friend fell by my side,
I'm sure I heard my sweet young daughter sigh,
So when that bullet took me down,
I simply lay there on the ground.

Knowing now my family were so close,
For me they would sound no last post,
With these three ladies by my side,
I knew from this battle, I would survive.

HOME AGAIN

To be home again with our kids to play,
Or just once more with the wife to lay,
Would it be wrong to be there and stay?

Must we be here, for we've no desire
To be crucified on that Boche barbed wire?
Nor trapped and drowned in a mud-stinking mire.

Stuck in this muddy, cold, miserable trench,
That same rusty wire as our fence,
A Lee Enfield Rifle our only defence.

Bullets and shells each day sent
To steal our young lives away,
So each man here has now learned to pray.

How can it be wrong,
For we've lingered here so long
To go home again where we belong?

Should we stay in this trench and surely be killed?
Or end our lives in a blood soaked field,
Just another Tommy buried on the side of a hill?

HANDS

Are these the hands
That held the gun,
And made me think
That war was fun?

Is this the hand
That squeezed the trigger,
And killed that man
With the boyish figure?

Are these the hands
That threw those bombs,
Till all those boys
Were dead and gone?

Are these the hands
That caress the ones I love,
Then clasp together
To praise the Lord above?

Is this the hand
That writes these lines?
Surely this hand
Cannot be mine?

THE VC

A Victoria Cross to win,
You must really be brave,
In the chaos of battle,
A comrade to save.

Destroy an enemy machine gun,
Perhaps while on the run,
Let your Captain know,
Through a mine field you would go.

Your enemy to pierce
With your bayonet so fierce,
Though big guns may rumble,
Be strong, never fumble.

To show your foe you are brave,
You must give them a wave,
Stand and shoot straight
Over your fallen mate.

A bullet may find your head,
Of course, you're sure to be dead,
So die happy not cross,
For someone else will now own your Victoria Cross.

ONCE A YEAR

They promised him glory, they promised him fame,
But at wars end he'd found nothing had changed,
Day after day for work he walked the street,
While at home his kids had little to eat.

They called him a hero when fighting that war,
While walking the streets they praised him no more,
Friends patted his back, said he'd done well,
Although they were not with him going through hell.

They plied him with medals his kids couldn't eat,
Then said he should stand on his own two feet,
Sadly from neglect he finally passed away,
Friends who had deserted him found little to say.

Now we proudly honour this hero
Once every year,
Then quickly forget him
The rest of the year.

A BATTALION SNIPER

An enemy will suffer such terrible fear,
When they sense our man is near,
For he has nerves forged from steel,
Cleverly stalking his foe with a will.

This man alone does patiently wait,
For a foe's one careless, fatal mistake,
Each squeeze he makes upon the trigger,
Will add yet another killing to the figure.

Our marksman is no fool,
He lives by one golden rule,
Take one shot from this cover,
Then swiftly move to another.

His work will bring no honour, nor joy,
When he clinically downs each single boy,
Still he will offer a fervent prayer,
For each Mother, whose son he leaves lying there.

His conscience will ever hold these numbers slain,
Though he may never know one single name,
His bullet does strike swift as a viper,
When the enemy meets our marksman, the battalion sniper.

DEAD IN A TRENCH

As we move down the line,
Men we met said they were fine,
They had been there for a year,
And had to suppress all their fear.

A year isn't so long,
Yet so many had gone
To that land far away,
With a brave patriotic display.

Fighting for country,
And for their King,
Yet when they left,
They went without a thing.

Many men stayed behind,
Their bodies none would find,
They rot with that barbed wire fence,
For they lay dead, in a trench.

CHRISTMAS EVE 1914

T'was Christmas Eve night,
A flare hissed through the sky,
Now the battlefield shone bright.

No machine gun did sound,
Nor soldier fall down,
No sergeant did yell,
Just someone singing 'The First Noel'.

Which seemed to float on the air,
From a lone soldier, in a trench just over there,
Many men would join in,
With that lone voice, singing that hymn.

Till the morning grew light,
On that field now devoid of all fight,
Where each man found a new friend,
Could this really mean the war's end?

Now 'that' Christmas has gone,
Yet that hymn still lingers on,
And so many years have now passed,
Oh such a pity that peace just didn't last.

DEAR FRIEND

Now my life is at an end,
Will you remember me?
My dear friend.

We fought together day by day,
Now the war is over,
And I must stay.

While you dear friend can live your life,
With adoring children
And loving wife.

From that lovely home, I know you will never stray,
But for me dear friend,
Each night please pray.

And when your life comes to a peaceful end,
I'll be waiting to greet you,
My dear friend.

THE SPIRIT BENEATH THE CROSS

A lone soldier knelt beneath an old cross,
And prayed for the many friends,
In battle he had lost.

Offering a prayer for each passing face,
Then knelt in silence,
As others took their place.

He prayed for those he did clearly see,
And wondered why
The Lord had taken all, yet not he.

As these thoughts began to wane,
He knew throughout this war,
Many dying men would ask the same.

Now kneeling silently beneath that old cross,
He offered just one more prayer,
For yet another soul he knew, now had been lost.

A SMALL WOODEN CROSS

Charging through a field of poppies
That sway all around,
And act as a cushion,
When each man is suddenly cut down.

Men screaming in agony,
Will slowly pass through,
They lay with cold staring eyes,
And a face covered with dew.

Men hurrying forward
Into machine gun and shell,
Had no idea this field
Was fashioned in hell.

Although they fought ever so bravely,
It has to be said,
They now rest with those poppies,
All of them dead.

So now each year, a Mother
Will lay a small wooden cross,
To mark the grave of a loved one,
She so sadly lost.

AUGUST 1914 WHY?

It was one hundred years ago this day,
Do we still remember those men
Who so bravely marched away?

Off to that war they had to go,
To defend old England,
Against a deadly foe.

We cheered with pride as they went,
But quickly forgot them,
When they were caught upon that barbed wire fence.

Now we pay them homage once a year,
Yet still forget dear Mothers
Who shed so many tears.

Today we praise those boys who went before,
But sadly we stand by and cry,
As our sons march into yet another war.

ONE LIFE

With only one life to live,
I've only one life to give,
A bullet this day
May take life away.

So will it then be said
I gave my all?
Maybe they'll say
I was just a fool.

Yet with this life
The war must end,
And I shall lie
Beside a friend.

Through another world
We shall roam,
Far away from
Our sweet home.

Now if this life
Was worth the living,
Can it be said
It was worth the giving?

A RIFLEMAN'S VERSE: THE SOMME 1916

"Time to go lads," the Captain did holler,
As his men stood watching the battle,
Filled with such horror,
But deep down inside,
He had no doubt, the Rifles would still follow.

As machine guns and shells began to sing,
Several of his men would feel their deadly sting,
Then they moved on,
The Captain rushed through a hollow,
Still knowing the brave Rifles would follow.

"Look lads," he cried, "we're among them now,"
Sadly men dying, could only wonder, but how?
Suddenly more bullets and many more shells
Put these men of the Rifles
On a field likened to hell.

The enemy now cheering, shouting and hollering,
Our Captain still knowing his Rifles were following,
Till finally a stray bullet at last found its mark,
Caught the brave Captain so close to his heart.

Now as their Captain lay slowly dying,
His men gathered round, some even crying,
Then a Rifleman looked down sobbing with sorrow,
"Don't worry Sir, we'll try again tomorrow."

On hearing these words,
The poor Captain knew,
Where he was now going,
His brave Riflemen surely would follow.

A MEDAL

They gave me a Medal, said it was great,
For killing those boys, when so full of hate.

Yes, I received a medal for shooting so good,
And killing two young boys in Delville Wood.

Folks patted my back, said I was grand,
Even the King shook my young hand.

They plied me with gifts, which I didn't enjoy,
For my brother's a soldier, and only a young boy.

Everyone said how brave, must have been fun,
Killing two young boys, with that rifle, my gun.

Some said it was great, you'll do better yet,
But those two boys I killed, I cannot forget.

Although a proud Rifleman, medal pinned to my breast,
Each night I pray for those boys, and wish them God bless.

THREE RIFLE SHOTS

High on a hillside so far away,
Is a long forgotten solitary grave,
Where an unknown soldier forever will lay,
He fell in battle one bright sunny day.

So they buried him deep
On that lonely hillside,
Within sound of a bugle calling close by,
And three rifle shots, high into the sky.

This soldier had a Mother,
Father and wife,
Now each one of them will grieve for that boy,
The rest of their life.

DISALLUSIONED

Heaven must be a lonely place,
For no-one dies here, with a smile on his face.

Heaven must be so very sparse and so bare,
For so many spirits still linger down here.

A heavenly spot must be so hard to obtain,
When you're blown to bits in the pouring rain.

Heaven must be a place where only God can dwell,
Because us boys in this trench are already in hell.

THE ANGELS OF MONS

The day had just begun,
When came shells from their big guns.
Our soldiers could no longer hold
Against an enemy, so brave, so bold.

They were forced to pull back,
As the night sky began to turn black,
Quite suddenly the cloud did part all around
And a bright light there, shone gloriously down.

On that field of battle all fighting there did cease,
For our Lord had declared, there must be peace.
The enemy reeled back in such terrible fear,
As the 'angels of Mons' did suddenly appear.

First English bowmen formed a line between
Those two belligerent armies that could be seen,
Then ghostly knights in armour appeared upon the scene.

Today we believe the Lord must have sent
Those spiritual 'angels of Mons',
For more bloodshed there to prevent.

Yet the slaughter throughout that war would go on,
And those 'angels of Mons'
Never did appear, in that battle, of 'The Somme'.

THOSE LEFT BEHIND

Was so silent, so clear, the wind very light,
All bayonets fixed,
The time was now right.

A field full of poppies, bursting into flower,
Like the boys marching through them,
All would be dead in an hour.

The poppies will re-bloom ever so well,
But the boys who passed through them
Had their first taste of hell!

So many wounded boys were quickly shipped home,
Yet still on that battlefield,
So many lost spirits forever must roam.

Part 2 – Second World War

For obvious reasons I have made a separate section for the Second World War. I should mention that, in some cases, I was involved in some of the incidents mentioned in a few of these verses, for example, 'The Blitz', the 'Train Guard', 'The Spitfire', 'Battle of Britain' and various others.

I have also taken the liberty of adding two more verses at the very end of this book, which have nothing to do with the First or Second World War. They are 'Titanic 1912' and 'A Forgotten Nurse'.

It only leaves me to hope you enjoy the Second World War verses as much as I hope you did the First World War verses.

Ronald Cove

DUNKIRK – MAY 1940

From shell ravished fields,
Over long sloping hills,
Our troops had to come,
In groups or maybe just ones,
So many men hurt,
Just to reach that war-torn town,
Called Dunkirk.

Though our army was weak,
Yet fought on for more than a week,
Through mist and through murk,
To reach those blood-soaked sands,
Of Dunkirk.

Enemy planes overhead,
Showing no mercy, it has to be said,
While others would stay, in the heavens and lurk,
Over those blood-soaked sands,
Of Dunkirk.

Sailors and men in small boats,
Found they had no time for jokes,
Certainly no time to shirk,
In saving the soldiers now trapped,
On those blood-soaked sands,
Of Dunkirk.

Our air force knew only too well,
Our boys on the beach were going through hell,
For they were but a few, so they dare not flirt,
Over those blood-soaked sands,
Of Dunkirk.

The rear guard put up a great fight,
Which went on by day and by night,
They'd never think to desert,
Those brave boys that were trapped,
On those blood-soaked sands,
Of Dunkirk.

Men were lined in the sea,
T'was so painful to see,
By friends on the shore,
Who so clearly saw,
When a mate would just sink with a sudden jerk,
Into the sea, off those blood-soaked sands,
Of Dunkirk.

Now it's all over, was it just fate,
Or perhaps a strange quirk,
That saved so many brave men,
From those blood-soaked sands,
Of Dunkirk.

RETURN FROM DUNKIRK

For the dirt on his face,
He felt no disgrace,
It showed he'd been
To that terrible place.

Why would he care,
About the sand in his hair,
It showed he'd really been there.

His anger so extreme,
By the pain he had seen,
Yet he stood tall,
Well, didn't they all?

They bore wounds
That still hurt,
These soldiers just back,
From a place called Dunkirk.

HIGH ON A HILL

When in battle lines you have formed,
Then you wait for the whistle to blow,
You may sense a spirit beside you,
A rifleman from the past long ago.

They fought in past battles,
All dressed in dark green,
These men of the rifles,
You never have seen.

As the Battalion moves forward,
They'll still act as your guide,
Don't ever doubt them,
These spirits that walk by your side.

If you should falter, along the way,
Brave comrades falling,
All around you,
You'll surely hear one of them say.

"Brace up my lad,
Remember your rifleman's skills,
Your lost comrades are now watching
O'er you, high on a hill."

A bullet may find you,
You might even be killed.
Still there'll be old comrades,
To meet you, high on the hill.

The battle is over,
Just where did they go,
Those men dressed in green,
From the past, long ago?

You knew they were with you,
To strengthen your will,
It's suddenly clear they're greeting new comrades,
High on that hill.

Then you grow old, no more doctors or pills,
Close your eyes, you will see
Comrades ready to greet you,
High on a hill.

THE LAST POST

Join the army, go to war,
You'll hear bugle calls
You've never heard before,
There's one for breakfast, dinner and tea,
Yet another to call each company.

A call in the morning,
Which will hurt your head,
One at night to see you to bed,
Now it has to be said,
They save the best one, for when you are dead.

So as we go through this war,
Just how many more,
Will give up the ghost,
Making his mates stand and listen,
As a bugler plays the last post?

AN OLD SOLDIER'S EYES

A gentle old man, you may first surmise,
Until you look deep into his now watery eyes,
You will learn of happiness, laughter and joy,
This old man lost, when only a boy.

All replaced by the slaughter,
Carnage, and the mayhem of war,
Of the comrades he lost in battle,
The fear, and oh, so many things more!

They will tell of hatred,
The cruelty this man has seen,
And of men dying in agony,
In a place they should never have been.

Yes, look deep into those eyes, where happiness once dwelled,
Until he walked into battle and straight into hell,
See the sorrow that will haunt him forever more,
There you will see an old soldier still haunted by war.

ONE OF THE FEW

He was just a young man dressed in light blue,
So proud of the spitfire, he so proudly flew.

Throughout the Battle of Britain he stood brave,
For it was England's fair land he did strive to save.

Now today when an aircraft does grace our sky,
Is it that Spitfire we can still hear up there on high?

Today's aircraft may fly ever so fast,
But that old Spitfire still cannot be surpassed.

And that young man dressed in light blue,
Will forever be remembered as one of the few.

THE SPITFIRE

A lone Spitfire dived out of a cloud one sunny day,
To engage an enemy formation heading our way,
The pilot so brave although very young,
He manoeuvred his aircraft to engage each single one,
In a Spitfire so sleek, fast and new,
He attacked each enemy bomber that came into view.

The brave enemy pilots could only look on in awe,
As straight towards them, this Spitfire did soar,
Then ever so smoothly banked out of sight,
As other Spitfires happily joined in the fight,
A squadron of Messerschmitts circling on high,
Finally met their match when these Spitfires,
With guns blazing struck, and swiftly rolled by.

All of this happened many years in the past,
Yet even today that name 'Spitfire' proudly still lasts,
Now when you hear a jet fighter roar by,
It's really the spirit of those Spitfire boys,
Still guarding our skies.

AN ICON

Each one an icon that graced our sky,
Every Spitfire that flew up there on high.

For us who watched them leave the ground,
There came a sweet purring Merlin engine sound.

Was the year 1940 our Spitfires' work first begun,
Now we owe those boys a debt, each single one.

When their guns first came into play,
An enemy plane would swiftly bank then slip away.

As those deadly bombers crossed over our shores,
A spitfire would greet them, whether one or a score.

As the blitz finally came to an end,
Those Spitfire boys had now grown into men.

Then they shipped them away to a foreign shore,
But still we remember that icon, the Spitfire, that War.

TO FORGET

What kind of country is this,
A soldier may die and never be missed?

What kind of people have we become,
To forget these men when their job is done?

Are they empty vessels that fight our fight,
Doomed to be maimed and die through the night?

Is it right they go on, paying the price,
While we stand by, our blood like ice?

How long must they go on killing, for you and for me?
Surely the good Lord didn't mean this to be?

Or is it because we think we're so great
They should give their lives, just for our sake?

Must they stay on the fields of war?
For it's certain we won't see the likes of these men any more.

UNIFORM AND FREEDOM

They joined the army and went to war,
Dressed in a uniform like their forefathers wore.

But back in the country they bravely fought for,
They fear to wear that uniform any more.

Although for freedom these men did fight,
It's clear to see they've been robbed of that right.

To proudly wear khaki in England's fair land,
Because of the hatred amongst their fellow man.

BATTLE OF BRITAIN

Our soldiers brought back from Dunkirk,
They felt well and truly done in,
Our great leader told us,
The battle of Britain must now begin.

Our army in tatters,
Not much they could do,
So we turned to our pilots,
And steadfast ground crews.

We watched them from the streets,
And fields from afar,
Heroes we called them,
They surely still are.

They fought high in the heavens,
Young men honest and true,
They fought so hard, for me and for you,
So sad to say they were only a few.

Day after Day,
They fought in our skies,
Mothers and Sweethearts
Would praise them with tears in their eyes.

They put up a great fight,
Those boys in light Blue,
Yet we down below,
Could never guess, just what they went through.

Now how do we thank them,
For so many have gone to their rest,
Let's all join together and say thank you,
Then whisper God Bless.

THE FORGOTTEN RIFLEMEN OF CALAIS

The Rifles were called into action one day,
Shipped over to the French port of Calais,
To engage German armour threatening Dunkirk,
Where brave comrades lay trapped,
Wounded and hurt.

The 60th Rifles, that regiment of old,
Their cap badge simply said 'Swift and Bold',
The 95th Rifles, their motto known to all,
'First man in, last man out' their rallying call,
The Queen Victoria Rifles went through such hell,
Fighting against armour until they, too, finally fell.

Now you may think of Dunkirk,
Our troops paying such a terrible price,
But spare a thought for Calais,
Those Rifles, that desperate fight,
For they too made that supreme sacrifice.

MALTA

Today Malta we visit, to have a good time,
Yet step back to the forties, just what do we find.
Although a small island, set in the sun,
They fought for survival, with very few guns.

The garrison stood steadfast, week after week,
Skimpy supplies, and very little to eat.
They waited for ships, that never would come,
Each night men would sleep by the side of an anti-aircraft gun.

Watching for Spitfires that never arrived,
Only Boche aircraft lurked there in the sky,
A squadron of Beaufighters one day broke through showing such
piloting skill,
The garrison happy to greet them, then fought on with a will.

Sixty Spitfires finally landed with a great show,
The enemy aircraft, just where did they go?
Those Spitfires entered the battle with well-loaded guns,
And waited for the foe to dive out of the sun.

Today the island holds the famed Malta Cross,
For bravery and causing Rommel that great desert loss,
That finished the war for that famed Africa Korps.

A FEAR OF MINES

As each night we walk the line,
We live in fear of a hidden mine.

For he who takes that fatal step, won't be coming back,
And should it be 'stand to' for an enemy attack,
Each man will wonder where to flee,
For he thinks 'that one' not coming back, may well be he.

"Don't worry about the mines" the Corporal said,
"Because while you're searching for a mine,
A sniper will put one through your head."

Then a chill runs up your spine
As a flare soars through the night,
You start to think: "Why am I here, this can't be bloody right."

Still we muddle through the dark, back where we belong,
Only to be told your lot has upped and bloody gone.
While we've been out all night, dodging bullets, shells and mines,
The buggers have pulled out, leaving us silly sods behind.

This leaves us no option than to retreat along another line,
And hope to god we don't step upon a British bloody mine.

THE LAST FIGHT

"Look!" a young Irishman cried,
When a lone German bomber
Fell from the sky.

Then those Irish Rifles had to go,
To fight the same foe
Their Fathers had fought so long ago.

Was 1940, late in September,
Folks from the Sportsman Inn will remember,
Two Spitfires had sealed the fate
Of that lone Junkers 88.

It came down on Graveney Marsh,
Although it was harsh,
Was to be the crew's last flight,
Still they put up a grand fight,
Till the Rifles crawled through a small dyke.

Then to the Sportsman Inn,
For a pint they all went,
Fliers and Riflemen in Seasalter,
Whitstable, Kent.

A SMALL BOAT FROM DUNKIRK

A small, lonely boat, drifting away from Dunkirk,
Six Tommies aboard all tired and hurt.

They were caught in a battle, of course we all knew,
Although many were saved, we lost quite a few.

An unknown sailor aboard, steering them free,
He prayed: "Oh Lord, how can this be?"

Out in mid ocean alone with his fear,
An enemy bomber did suddenly appear.

Just one bomb sent that little boat down,
And until this day, no one's ever been found.

Now at night when the sea breeze softly sighs,
Six Mothers at home will unashamedly cry.

As for that sailor who tried his very best,
We can only hope, by the Lord, he was heavenly blessed.

THE SPIRITS OF NEPAL

Was in Delhi alongside the 60th Rifles,
They fought as a team,
Now like the 60th they too,
Dress in rifleman green.

While in the desert at El Alamein,
They were to stand with our Rifles,
To fight, and to die, once again.

In so many foreign fields with the 60th,
They have stood time and again,
And like the good friends they are,
They stood through to the end of every campaign,
And never once did we hear them complain.

Now if at night you carefully study the sky,
You may see many a regiment quickly march by,
But the ones wearing dark green will march proudest of all,
For they are the Gurkha, our friends from Nepal.

Then if you stand ever so quietly,
You will hear a soft bugle call,
It's the 60th Rifles calling to the spirits of friends,
That now rest in Nepal.

THE TRAIN GUARD

On a train guard we went,
To a place called Berlin,
One Sergeant, three Riflemen,
And a Lieutenant thrown in.

We stopped at a Russian-held station,
Where they stood very tall,
Rifles, machine guns pointing our way,
Not nice at all.

No-one could get on or off,
So there wasn't a rush,
The Ruskies cocked their weapons,
Still pointing at us.

The Sergeant said: "Now boys
Just move to your right,"
"Why?" said a rifleman,
"We're still in their sights."

The Lieutenant yelled out:
"We're British you know,"
A Russian called back,
"Yes, and we want you to go."

At that moment things got really tricky,
It wasn't too hard to see,
They were taking the micky.

Our Officer nodded,
"Load five rounds," he declared,
"But don't point at the Ruskies,
Point your guns in the air."

What could we do?
Things were looking so grim,
A Sergeant, three Riflemen,
We just wasn't with him.

Twenty rounds between us,
How far would they go?
We'd fire one each,
And that's all we would know.

Common sense prevailed in the end,
For the driver backed the train
Out of sight, round a small bend.

Today you can visit Berlin,
The Brandenburgh Gate,
Yet one day on that station,
Five Riflemen didn't think it so great.

THE REGIMENTS

The King's Royal Rifles, a regiment of old,
Their cap badge declared them to be 'Swift and Bold',
Many Honours in battle they have won,
But one stroke of a pen cancelled out each single one.

The Rifle Brigade, a regiment known by all,
'First man in, Last man out' their rallying call,
Yes, that very same pen, sad to say,
Took that famous regiment call and cast it away.

The steadfast Black Watch,
That proud regiment of Scots,
Until that pen struck again,
Now they too have been robbed of all fame.

Who knows just how many other regiments we've lost
Since that rogue pen took over as boss,
Shall it continue writing until
It's buried all our regiments, high on that hill.

PHOTO OF GRANNY

It's only an old photo of Granny,
Which hangs on our living room wall,
Went all through the blitz,
And never once did it fall.

Although the bombs rained down,
For quite a while,
Dear Granny just hung there,
With a kind, tolerant smile.

One night when the bombing
Became so severe,
Her smile it changed,
And a defiant grin did suddenly appear.

Oh such a hard life Granny must have had,
Just a lonely old lady, which really is sad,
And for her stories we found no time at all,
But I'm sure she forgave us, for her smile
Still shines down from our living room wall.

THE BLITZ

London dear London, just what have they done?
With bombs, bright searchlights,
And those big, booming guns.

People in shelters shivering in fright,
Yet praying for peace, night after night,
Planes showering death down at a terrible rate,
No wonder old London was so full of hate.

At home they're nice fellows, of this there's no doubt,
But not over here, where they're bombing us out.
High in the heavens showing no pity,
They just seemed intent on ruining our city.

With bombs raining down, blowing old London to bits,
This was the time which is known as the blitz.

Mothers with babies, oh so much crying,
While old people are asking,
"Is our London dying?"

Now it's all over, the years have rolled on,
Most Londoners wonder,
Where their dear London's gone?

So if you were there, now one of the few,
You'll think of old London,
Just what did they do?

Of course they've rebuilt it, so bright and so new,
Yet old folks still remember,
The London they knew.

TITANIC – 1912

A sea so calm, many stars shone bright
As that ship cruised through that cold icy night,
A luxury liner on its maiden voyage that April day,
Far out at sea, a lone iceberg slowly drifting its way.

So many thought how lucky to be
On this beautiful ship, racing through a calm sea,
Sailing so fast on that fatal night,
When that berg silently drifted into sight.

It was to be full steam ahead,
As through that crisp night, onward they sped,
Suddenly there came an alarming shout,
Then the crew started swinging the few lifeboats out.

Women and children away in small boats,
For those still aboard, there wasn't much hope,
"But the ship's unsinkable," everyone said
As she slipped 'neath the waves, down by the head.

With passengers singing 'nearer my God to thee',
As that ship did falter, on that cold, calm sea,
The Captain declared, there must be no panic,
On that cold April night, when we lost the Titanic.

A FORGOTTEN NURSE

With decaying filth from the sewers everywhere,
And the stench of cholera, that fouled the air.

Still day after day the wounded they came,
To lie in Scutari that place of ill fame.

Although at times herself unwell,
She would comfort those soldiers where ever they fell.

From the Alma to Sebastopol as these men did fall,
This young nurse would readily answer their suffering call.

When that thin red line made that heroic stand,
The fallen found solace at this young nurse's hand.

With her lantern shining oh so bright,
Throughout those corridors each single night.

She tirelessly helped those wounded soldiers somehow,
So we should never forget that brave nurse, Florence Nightingale.